CAMELOT

Music by
FREDERICK LOEWE

Book and Lyrics by
ALAN JAY LERNER

Based on
The Once and Future King
by T. H. WHITE

Vocal Score

Edited by FRANZ ALLERS
Piano Reduction by TRUDE RITTMAN

ʜAPPELL MUSIC COMPANY

ɔr performance of this work, whether legitimate, stock,
ιateur, or foreign, should be addressed to:
TAMS-WITMARK
560 Lexington Avenue
New York, N.Y., 10022

CAMELOT

Produced by the Messrs. LERNER • LOEWE • HART
December 3, 1960 at the Majestic Theatre, New York City

Production Staged by
MOSS HART

Choreography and Musical Numbers by HANYA HOLM
Scenic Production by OLIVER SMITH
Costumes Designed by ADRIAN, AND TONY DUQUETTER
Lighting by FEDER
Musical Direction by FRANZ ALLERS
Orchestrations by ROBERT RUSSELL BENNETT AND PHILIP J. LANG
Dance and Choral Arrangements by TRUDE RITTMAN
Hair Styles by ERNEST ADLER

Cast of Characters
(In order of appearance)

SIR DINADAN	John Cullum
SIR LIONEL	Bruce Yarnell
MERLYN	David Hurst
ARTHUR	Richard Burton
GUENEVERE	Julie Andrews
NIMUE	Marjorie Smith
A PAGE	Leland Mayforth
LANCELOT	Robert Goulet
DAP	Michael Clarke-Laurence
PELLINORE	Robert Coote
CLARIUS	Richard Kuch
LADY ANNE	Christina Gillespie
A LADY	Leesa Troy
SIR SAGRAMORE	James Gannon
A PAGE	Peter de Vise
HERALD	John Starkweather
LADY CATHERINE	Virginia Allen
MORDRED	Roddy McDowall
SIR OZANNA	Michael Kermoya
SIR GWILLIAM	Jack Dabdo
MORGAN LE FEY	M'el D
TOM	Robin St

SINGERS: Joan August, Mary Sue Berry, Marnell Bruce, Judy H
Benita James, Marjorie Smith, Shelia Swenson, Leesa Troy,
White, Frank Bouley, Jack Dabdoub, James Gannon, Mur
kind, Warren Hays, Paul Huddleston, Michael Kermoya
Maloof, Larry Mitchell, Paul Richards, John Taliaferro.

DANCERS: Virginia Allen, Judi Allinson, Laurie Archer, Ca
Joan Coddington, Katia Geleznova, Adriana Kea
Mitchell, Claudia Schroeder, Beti Seay, Jerry Bowers,
Randy Doney, Richard Englund, Richard Gain, Gene
Kirby, Richard Kuch, Joe Nelson, John Starkw
Tarbutton.

CAMELOT

Synopsis of Scenes

ACT I

SCENE 1: A HILLTOP NEAR CAMELOT
A long time ago

SCENE 2: NEAR CAMELOT
Immediately following

SCENE 3: ARTHUR'S STUDY
Five years later

SCENE 4: A ROADSIDE NEAR CAMELOT
A few months later

SCENE 5: A PARK NEAR THE CASTLE
Immediately following

SCENE 6: A TERRACE OF THE CASTLE
A few weeks later

SCENE 7: THE TENTS OUTSIDE THE JOUSTING FIELD
A few days later

SCENE 8: THE GRANDSTAND OF THE FIELD

SCENE 9: THE TENTS OUTSIDE THE JOUSTING FIELD
Immediately following

SCENE 10: THE TERRACE
Two years later

SCENE 11: THE CORRIDOR LEADING TO THE GREAT HALL
Immediately following

SCENE 12: THE GREAT HALL
Immediately following

ACT II

SCENE 1: THE CASTLE GARDEN
A few years later

SCENE 2: THE TERRACE
A few weeks later

SCENE 3: NEAR THE FOREST OF MORGAN LE FEY
A few days later

SCENE 4: THE FOREST OF MORGAN LE FEY
Immediately following

SCENE 5: CORRIDOR
That night

SCENE 6: THE QUEEN'S BEDCHAMBER
Immediately following

SCENE 7: CAMELOT
Several days later

SCENE 8: A BATTLEFIELD NEAR JOYOUS GARD
A few weeks later

ORIGINAL INSTRUMENTATION: Flute/*Piccolo,* Oboe/*English Horn,* B♭ Clarinet, B♭ Clarinet/*E♭ Clarinet/Bass Clarinet/Flute,* Bassoon; 3 Horns, 3 Trumpets, 2 Trombones; 2 Percussion, Guitar/*Lute/Mandolin,* Harp; 10 Violins, 2 Violas, 2 Violoncellos, 2 Basses.

Musical Program

ACT I

ACT II

CAMELOT
Overture

No. 1

FREDERICK LOEWE

The curtain rises

SIR DINADAN: My Sainted Mother!...
Dialogue continues over tremolo.
CUE TO END:
MERLYN:...Does that solve it?

March

Cue: SIR DINADAN:... at the foot of the hill in traditional fashion.

No.3 I Wonder What The King Is Doing Tonight

ALAN JAY LERNER

FREDERICK LOEWE

Cue: ARTHUR: ... That's precisely what you are doing. Every last blessed one of you.

Lyrics:
I know what my peo-ple are think-ing to night, As home through the shad-ows they wan - der. Ev -'ry-one smil-ing in se-cret de -light, They stare at the cas-tle and pon - der. When- ev - er the wind blows this way, _____ You can al-most hear ev-'ry-one

won-der what the King is up to to-night? How

goes the fi-nal ho-ur As he sees the bri-dal bow-er Be-ing

le-gal-ly and re-gal-ly pre-pared? Well, I'll

tell you what the King is do-ing to-night: He's

99 oc - cu - pies his time while wait - ing for the bride? He's

search - ing high and low for some place to hide. And

107 oh, the ex - pec - ta - tion, The sub - lime an - tic - i - pa - tion He must

feel a - bout the wed - ding night to come! Well! I'll

tell you what the King is feel - ing to - night: He's

numb! He shakes! He quails! He

quakes! Oh, that's what the King is do - ing to -

night!

Segue

The Simple Joys Of Maidenhood

GUENEVERE comes running on, as if being pursued.

18 Moderato

St. Gen - e - vieve! St. Gen - e - vieve! It's Guen - e - vere! Re - mem - ber me? St. Gen - e - vieve! St. Gen - e - vieve! I'm o - ver here be - neath this tree. You know how faith - ful and de - vout I am. You must ad - mit I've al - ways been a lamb. But Gen - e - vieve, St. Gen - e - vieve, I

No.5

Camelot

Cue: ARTHUR: Ordained by decree!

...Extremely uncommon.

GUENEVERE: Oh, come now.

ARTHUR: It's true! It's true! The crown has made it clear:— The cli-mate must be per-fect all the year.— A law was made a dis-tant moon a-go here, Ju-ly and Au-gust can-not be too hot; And

Guenevere's Welcome

Cue: SIR DINADAN: There she is!
GUENEVERE: Wart, please....

Cue: ARTHUR:... And since I am, I have been ill at ease in my crown. Until I dropped from the tree and my eyes beheld you.

65

73

ARTHUR:... War would have been declared. GUENEVERE: War?

Vls.

+Gtr.

Vc.

Bsn.

Over me? How simply marvelous! +W.W., Hns.

Allegro con spirito
W.W. Bells 8va

rit *molto cresc.* Hp. gliss.

f a tempo
Tutti

Tbns.

81

brillante

W.W., Vls.
Bells 8va

Tpts.

(Dialogue)

Hns.

sffz

Cue: MERLYN:...One year... two years...what does it matter? I can see a night five years from now...

34 and Guenevere! Did I warn him of Lancelot and Guenevere?........ And Mordred?.......

Mordred!...... I didn't warn him of Mordred, and I must!.......

42

I remember nothing of Lancelot and Guenevere.... And Mordred!....
etc.

It's all gone... My magic is gone.

49

(off stage) SOLO

On-ly you, On-ly I, World fare-well, World good-bye. To our

Ah _____ Ah _____ To our

Ah _____ Ah _____ To our

WOMEN'S VOICES

Poco meno mosso

home 'neath the sea We shall fly, Fol - low me.

home 'neath the sea We shall fly.

MERLYN:

58 Goodbye, Arthur. My memory of the future is gone. I know no more the sorrows and joys before you

I can only wish for you in ignorance, like everyone else.

Reign long and reign happily.

Oh, and Wart — remember to think!

(Dialogue)

No.9

End Of Study Scene

Cue: GUENEVERE: It's marvelous.

ARTHUR: Yes, it is. It's marvelous. Absolutely marvelous. Page, give the signal.

PAGE: Yes, your Majesty.

No. 10   *Countryside near Camelot.*

C'est Moi

Piano

Tempo rubato
LANCELOT:

all that and more I shall be! _____ A

33 Alla marcia

knight of the ta - ble round should be in - vin - ci - ble; Suc -
soul of a knight should be a thing re - mark - a - ble: His

ceed where a less fan - tas - tic man would fail; _____ Climb a
heart and his mind as pure as morn - ing dew. _____ With a

41

wall no one else can climb; Cleave a drag - on in rec - ord time; Swim a
will and a self - re - straint That's the en - vy of ev - 'ry saint, He could

moat in a coat of heav-y i-ron mail. _____ No
eas-i-ly work a mir-a-cle or two! _____ To

49

mat-ter the pain he ought to be un-winc-a-ble, Im-
love and de-sire he ought to be un-spark-a-ble. The

poss-i-ble deeds should be his dai-ly fare. But
ways of the flesh should of-fer no al-lure. But

57

where in the world Is there in the world A A
where in the world Is there in the worlá A A

man so extra - or - di - naire? _____
man so un touch'd and pure? _____

W.W.
Str.
en dehors

Bsn., Hn., Vc.

67 Allegretto scherzando

*(Spoken
modestly) C'est moi...C'est moi! C'est moi, I blush to dis - close, I'm
C'est moi! C'est moi, I'm forced to ad - mit! 'Tis

W.W., Str., Hp.

p

I, I hum - bly re - ply. _____ That mor - tal who These
far too no - ble to lie. _____ That man in whom These

(♪ = ♪)

mar - vels can do, C'est moi, C'est moi, 'tis I! _____ I've
qual - i - ties bloom, C'est moi, C'est moi, 'tis I! _____ I've

Fl., Cl.

mp

*)2nd stanza only

91

moi! C'est moi, So ad - mir - 'bly fit; A
moi! C'est moi, The an - gels have chose To

mf W.W. Hns., Str. div.

French Pro - me - theus un - bound. _____ And here I stand with
fight their bat - tles be - low. _____ And here I stand as

Tbns.
Timp.

val - or un - told, Ex - cept - ion - 'lly brave, a - maz - ing - ly bold, To
pure as a pray'r, In - cred - i - bly clean, with vir - tue to spare, The

*)

99

1. **2.**

serve at the Ta - ble Round! The
god - li - est man I know! C'est moi!

+Tbns. *ff* Tutti *ff* Tutti

*)*Bars 97 and 98 are rit. in the 2nd stanza.*

The Lusty Month Of May
(Dance And Song)

Cue: ARTHUR:... Welcome, Lancelot. Bless you for coming, and welcome to the table. *(The scene changes.)*

151 Allegretto giocoso

la! It's May! The lust-y month of May! That love-ly month when ev-'ry-one goes Bliss-ful-ly a-stray. Tra

159

la! It's here! That shock-ing time of year! When tons of wick-ed lit-tle thoughts mer-ri-ly ap-pear. It's

228

May!   It's May!   The month of "yes you may,"   The

S.

Tra   la   Tra   la

A.

Tra   la   Tra   la

T.

Tra   la   Tra   la

228

Fl.

Bsn.Vc.

time   for   ev - 'ry   friv - o - lous whim,   Prop - er or "im." It's

colla voce   rit

GUENEVERE:

Tra

No.11a   Pellinore's Entrance

End Of Scene

Cue: SIR LIONEL: He shall have my challenge in the morning.

GUENEVERE: Thank you, Sir Lionel.

SIR SAGRAMORE: And mine.

GUENEVERE: Thank you, Sir Sagramore.

SIR DINADAN: And mine.

Change Of Scene

How To Handle A Woman

Cue: GUENEVERE:... let him command me! And Yours Humbly will graciously obey. What? What? *(She exits)*

ARTHUR: What?

Blast!

Blast you, Merlyn!

This is all your fault!

And what of teach-ing me by turn-ing me to an-i-mal and bird, From beav-er to the small-est bob-o-link!

I should have had a whirl At chang-ing to a girl, To

did he not give coun-sel and say... What was it now? My mind's a

wall. Oh, yes! By jove, now I re-call:

57 Moderato

How to han-dle a wom-an? There's a way, said the wise old man;

A way known by ev - 'ry wom-an Since the

94

Tent Scene

The Tumblers

No.16

Cue: SIR DINADAN:... How benevolent. Do you know what I shall be thinking, Lancelot, when I see you on your horse? There he is, the Sermon on the mount.

The Jousts

Change Of Scene

Before I Gaze At You Again

Cue: ARTHUR: It might do you good to get away from Round Tables and chivalry for a little while. Don't you think?
(GUENEVERE does not answer)
Don't you think? *(She still doesn't answer. He turns and exits.)*
GUENEVERE: Oh, Lance, go away...

Cue: ARTHUR:... all borders will disappear...and all the things I dreamed... I dreamed... I dreamed.   *(Curtain)*
The scene changes to a corridor in the Castle.

Allegro, poco sostenuto

Piano

ARTHUR: Excalibur!

75 **Andante con moto**

SIR DINADAN: To be invested Knights of the Round Table of England: of Brackley... Colgrevance.

(Colgrevance steps forward

and is knighted.) Of Winchester... Bliant.

83

(Bliant steps forward and is knighted.) Of Wales... Guilliam.

(Guilliam steps forward and is knighted.) Of Cornwall...Castor. *(Castor steps forward and is knighted.)*

91

Of Joyous Gard:
Lancelot Du Lac.

(Lancelot steps forward. ARTHUR hesitates, then he knights Lancelot.)

ARTHUR: *(alone in the Great Hall)* Proposition: If I could choose, from every

woman who breathes on this earth, the face I would most love, the smile, the touch, the voice, the heart, the laugh, the soul itself, every detail and feature to the smallest strand of hair - they would all be Jenny's.

+Fl., Cl.

dolce

141 Proposition: If I could choose, from every man who breathes on this earth, a man for my brother

and a man for my son, a man for my friend, they would all be Lance.

+Hp.

149 Yes, I love them. I love them, and they answer me again with pain and torment. Be it sin or not sin, they betray

(Fl.)   (Str.)

(Bs. Cl.)

me in their hearts, and that's far sin enough. I see it in their eyes and feel it when they speak, and they must pay for

+Bsn.

Cl.

it and be punished. I shan't be wounded and not return it in kind. I'm done with feeble hoping. I demand a man's vengeance.

161 Poco più grave

Proposition: I'm a King, not a man. And a civilized King. Could it

possibly be civilized to destroy what I love? Could it possibly be civilized to love myself above all?

169 What of their pain and their torment? Did they ask for this calamity? Can passion be selected?

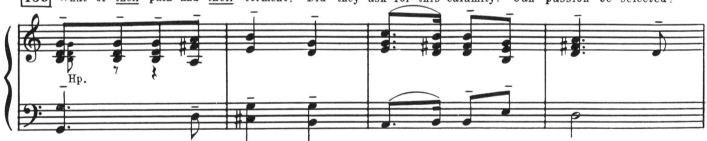

Is there any doubt of their devotion... to me, or to our Table?

Entr'acte

No. 22
Madrigal And "If Ever I Would Leave You"

They leave.

Str.,Cl.

poco a poco

Hp.

25 Moderato LANCELOT: *(Sings a madrigal to GUENEVERE.)*

Tou - jours j'ai eu le mê - me voeux, Sur terre une dé - es - se, au

mf Str.,Lute, Hp.

+Bsn.

31 ciel un Dieu. Un hom - me dé - sire pour êt - re heu - reux Sur terre une dé - es - se, au

Hn.

+W.W.

ciel un Dieu. Years may come; years may go; This, I know, will e'er be so: The

Hp.,Lute

rea-son to live is on-ly to love A god-dess on earth and a God a-bove.

Str., Lute, Hp. +W.W. Vl. Solo

GUENEVERE: Did you write that, Lance?

LANCELOT: GUENEVERE: LANCELOT:
Yes. Why do you always write about you? I can't write about you.
Why don't you ever write about me? I love you too much. Jenny, I should leave you,

Lute Solo
Str. (Soli)

and never come back. I've said it to myself day after day, year after year. But how can I? Look at you. When

Str. (Tutti) poco rit. +Hp. Hp.

If Ever I Would Leave You

Con espressione

would I? *(He sings)*

If ev - er I would leave you _____ It would-n't be in

Fl. Cls.

mf Str.

No. 23

The Seven Deadly Virtues

Cue: ARTHUR: The adage "blood is thicker than water", was invented by undeserving relatives. *(He exits)*
MORDRED: Virtue and proper deeds, Your Majesty, like what?

Change Of Scene

No.25   What Do The Simple Folk Do?

Cue: GUENEVERE: Royalty never can. Why is that, Arthur? Other people do. They seem to have ways and means of finding respite. What do they do? Farmers, cooks, blacksmiths.....

33

do _____ We do not? _____

+Bsn., Hns.

ARTHUR: *(seriously)*

I have been in-formed By those who know them well, They

W.W.
mf
Str., Hn.
etc.
Trgl.
Trgl.

41

find re-lief in quite a clev-er way. _____

+2 Hns.

Bsn.

When they're sore-ly pressed, They whis-tle for a spell; And

Trgl.
Trgl.

When all the dol - drums be - gin, _____ What

keeps each of them in his skin? _____ What

an - cient na - tive cus - tom Pro - vides the need - ed glow? Oh,

what _____ do sim - ple folk

tricks a roy - al high - ness Is min - us From birth. Bells

177 What then, I won - der do they _____ To

chase all the gob - lins a - way? _____ They

185 have some tri - bal sorc' - ry You have - n't men - tioned yet. Oh,

The Enchanted Forest

Queen Morgan Le Fey and her entourage enter.

No. 27

The Persuasion

Cue: MORGAN LE FEY: How do you know I build invisible walls?
MORDRED: Mummy told me. Please, dear aunt?
MORGAN: No, I will not harm little Wart. Court!

Fresh mar - zi - pan!

All yours it will be If you

build me a wee Lit - tle wall.

MORGAN:

Do you

184

ARTHUR: Sh-h-h. It's awfully quiet around here, isn't it? *(MORGAN appears and listens)* Not a leaf rustling, not a whisper in the woods..... It makes one feel rather drowsy. Would you care to rest a bit?

PELLINORE: No thank you, old man. I want to find that bird, what? I mean, if you hit a bird with an arrow, it ought to fall down like a gentleman. *(He exits)*

ARTHUR: Merlyn, do you remember how often we walked this valley when I was a boy?

Do you know what I miss of those days? Not my youth. My innocence. My innocence. *(He closes his eyes)*

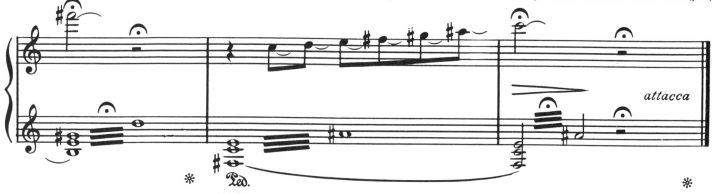

No. 28   The Invisible Wall

Morgan Le Fey's Court appears, carrying imaginary bricks. She directs the building of a wall around Arthur.

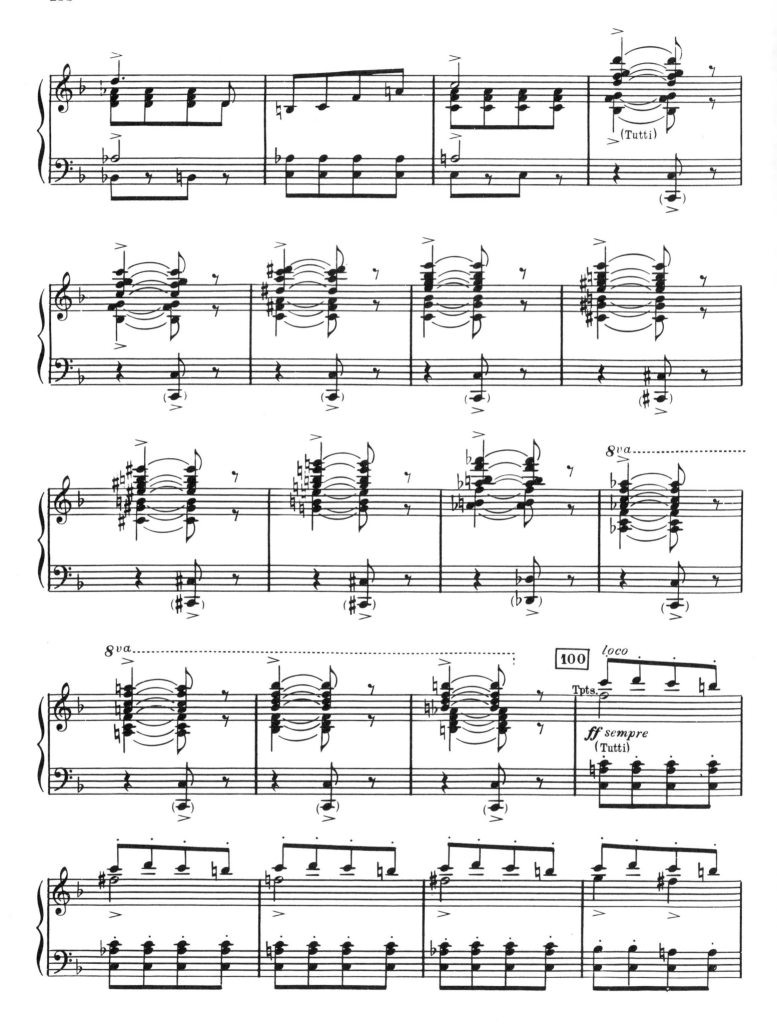

Morgan and her Court disappear.

No. 29   Change Of Scene

Cue: ARTHUR:... Find Lance. Find Jenny. Tell them to be careful.
PELLINORE: You know, Arthur?
ARTHUR: Do as I say, Pelly! *(PELLINORE exits)* Morgan Le Fey!

FIRST LADY-IN-WAITING:
Goodnight, Milady.

SECOND LADY-IN-WAITING:
Goodnight, Your Majesty.

Corridor Scene

FIRST LADY-IN-WAITING: Sleep well, Your Majesty.   *LANCELOT appears, looks*

Andante con moto

around   furtively   and   disappears   into   the   Queen's   chamber.

MORDRED appears from the other side, snaps his fingers. Several Knights enter. As he nods to them to follow

him, PELLINORE *enters.*   PELLINORE: Hey you!   MORDRED: The name is Mordred.   *(Dialogue continues)*

No.31 Change Of Scene And Incidental Music

Cue: MORDRED: Pellinore, in a little while, I shall be in charge of this Castle. And shortly after that, gentlemen, the Kingdom. *(Curtain)*

No. 32 # I Loved You Once In Silence

Cue: GUENEVERE: ... And suddenly we're less alone than ever.

LANCELOT: But why?

GUENEVERE: *(The music begins.)* Now that the people are gone, can't you see the shadow between us? It's wider than the sea.

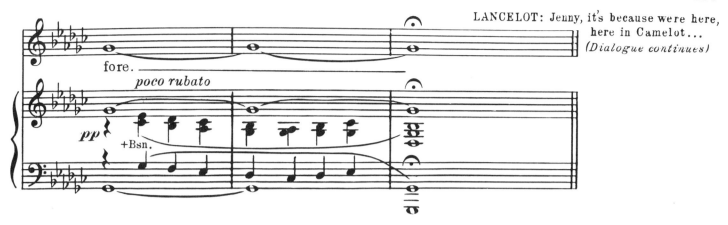

LANCELOT: Jenny, it's because we're here, here in Camelot...
(Dialogue continues)

fore.

poco rubato

GUENEVERE: ...What sort of heartbreaking solution is that?
LANCELOT: Forgive me, Jenny, *(The music begins.)*

L'istesso tempo

I shall never mention it again, I swear.

Nor shall I come to see you again. I swear that, too.

GUENEVERE: Lance? *(He stops)* Have we no more tender words to say to each other? *(She sings)*

The si — lence ___ at last was bro — ken! ___

No. 33
Guenevere

LANCELOT: If I escape, I shall come and rescue you. If I am killed, send word to Joyous Gard. Someone will come. *(The music begins)*
(He takes a menacing step forward. All stand in tableau—stillness. A chorus enters, wiping out the scene behind.)

sen - tenced _____ to the flame. _____ As the
dawn _____ filled the sky, _____ On the
day _____ she would die, _____ There was
won - der _____ far and near: _____ Would the

And the mo - ment _____ now was here _____

And the mo - ment _____ now was here _____

For the end of _____ Gue - ne - vere. _____

For the end of _____ Gue - ne - vere. _____

GUENEVERE enters. She is accompanied by a

And lo! A - head the ar - my, hold - ing a - loft his spear, Came

ARTHUR: Lance!

Lance - lot to save his dear Gue - ne - vere. _____

165 Lance! Come save her. HERALD: Shall I signal the torch, Your Majesty? DINADAN: *(rushing*

in) Arthur, an army from Joyous Gard is storming the gate. Shall I double the guard? Arthur, you're

inviting a massacre! *(He rushes off)* ARTHUR: Save her, Lance, save her!

As he res - cued ___ Gue - ne - vere. ___

As he res - cued ___ Gue - ne - vere. ___

Tpts.

cresc.

197 MORDRED: Sweet heaven, what a sight!

197

p sub.

Hns.
Tbns.
Str.

Can you see it from there Arthur? Can you see your goodly Lancelot

W.W.

Tpts.

Tutti

In the dy - ing ___ can - dle's gleam ___

In the dy - ing ___ can - dle's gleam ___

Came the sun - down ___ of a dream. ___

Came the sun - down ___ of a dream. ___

DINADAN: (*entering*) Most of the guard is killed, Arthur, and over eighty knights. They're heading for the Channel. I'll make ready the army to follow. Arthur, we want revenge! *(He exits)*

ARTHUR: Oh God, is it all to start again? Is my

almighty fling at peace to be over so soon? Am I back where I began? Am I? Am I?

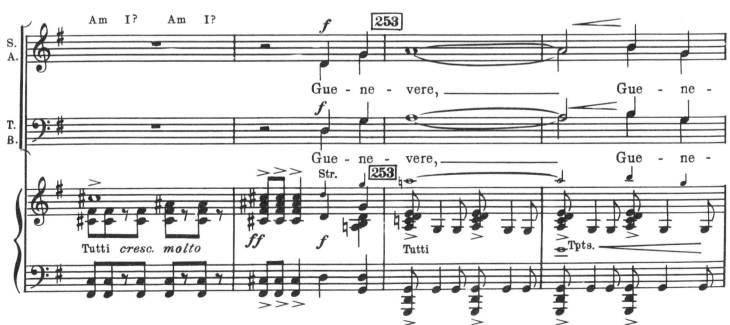

Gue - ne - vere, _____ Gue - ne -

Gue - ne - vere, _____ Gue - ne -

No. 34   Battle Call

Cue: ARTHUR:... Something you cannot taste or touch, smell or feel; without substance, life, reality or memory.

No. 35   Farewell

Cue: LANCELOT: Is there nothing to be done?

ARTHUR: Nothing, but play out the game and leave the decisions to God. Now go.

ARTHUR: You must go, too, Jenny.   GUENEVERE: I know. So often in the past I would look up in your eyes

and there I would find forgiveness. Perhaps one day in the future it shall be there again. But I won't be with you....

I won't see it.   *(He takes her in his arms.)*   Oh, Arthur, Arthur, I see

what I wanted to see.   ARTHUR: Goodbye, my love...*(GUENEVERE leaves him.)* My dearest love. *(He hears a rustling behind the tent.)* Who's there? *(Dialogue continues.)*

No. 36   Finale Ultimo

Cue: ARTHUR: And for as long as you live you will remember what I, the King, tell you; and you will do as I command.
       TOM: Yes, Milord.

17

Ask ev'-ry per-son if he's heard the sto - ry, _____

pp   + Bsn.

And tell it strong and clear if he has not:

Fl.   Hns.

25

That once there was a fleet-ing wisp of glo - ry _____

Called Ca - me - lot.

W. W. 8va

Hns.   *mf*   Tpts.

My teacher Merlyn, who always remembered things that haven't happened

better than things that have, told me once that a few hundred years from now it will be discovered

that the world is round... round like the table at which we sat with such high hope and

noble purpose. If you do what I ask, perhaps people will remember how we of

Camelot went questing for right and honor and justice. Perhaps one day men will sit around

Excalibur, I knight you Sir Tom of Warwick. And I command you to return home and carry out

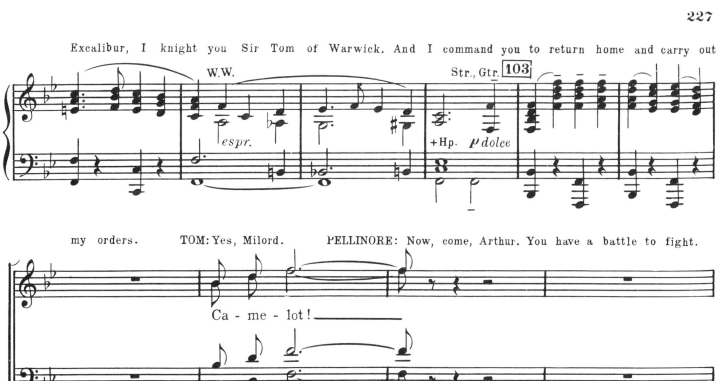

my orders.　TOM: Yes, Milord.　PELLINORE: Now, come, Arthur. You have a battle to fight.

ARTHUR: Battle? I've won my battle, Pelly. Here's my victory! What we did will be remembered.

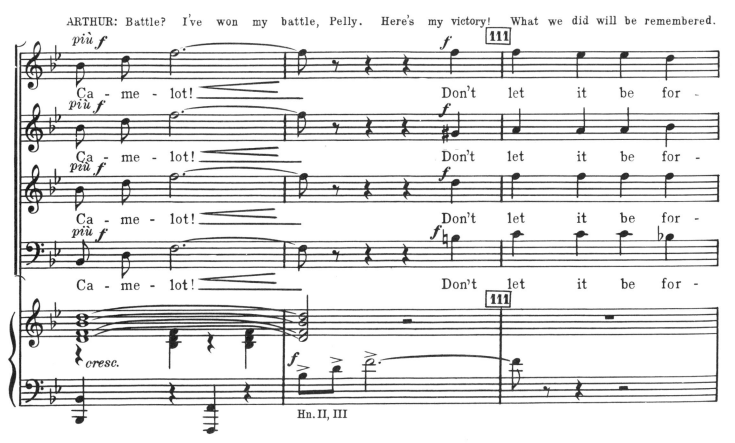

228

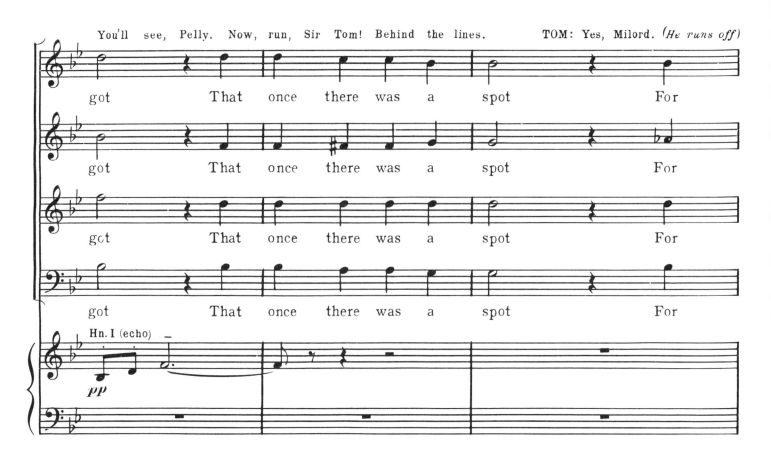

You'll see, Pelly. Now, run, Sir Tom! Behind the lines.   TOM: Yes, Milord. *(He runs off)*

got   That   once   there   was   a   spot   For

got   That   once   there   was   a   spot   For

got   That   once   there   was   a   spot   For

got   That   once   there   was   a   spot   For

Hn. I (echo)

pp

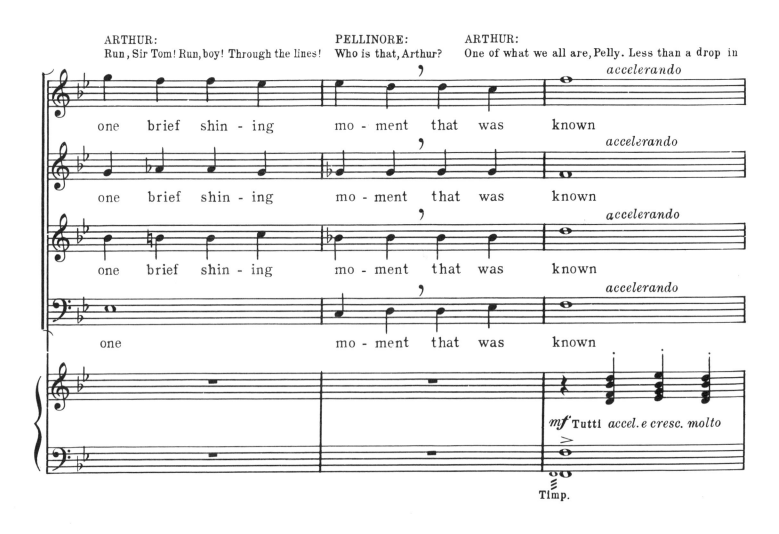

ARTHUR:
Run, Sir Tom! Run, boy! Through the lines!   PELLINORE: Who is that, Arthur?   ARTHUR: One of what we all are, Pelly. Less than a drop in

accelerando

one   brief   shin - ing   mo - ment   that   was   known

accelerando

one   brief   shin - ing   mo - ment   that   was   known

accelerando

one   brief   shin - ing   mo - ment   that   was   known

accelerando

one   mo - ment   that   was   known

mf **Tutti** *accel. e cresc. molto*

Timp.

the great blue motion of the sunlit sea. But it seems some of the drops sparkle, Pelly.　Some of them do sparkle!

(The curtain falls slowly)

Largo

ff Tutti

poco rit.

fff

No.37 Music For Curtain Calls And Exit

Piano